MW01614680

Surviving Uncertainty

Surviving Uncertainty

Taking a Hero's Journey

by Lane Wallace

© 2009, 2012 Lane Wallace. All rights reserved.
First published in 2009. Second edition 2012

ISBN 978-0-9853446-1-0

Published by:
No Map. No Guide. No Limits.
P.O. Box 171
Marblehead, MA 01945

 no map. no guide. no limits.®

WWW.NOMAPNOGUIDENOLIMITS.COM

Designed by: Susanne Weihl | Folio 2
Cover photo © iStockphoto.com/RelaxFoto.de
Illustrations © 2012 Tyler McDaniel

"This time, like all times, is a very good one, if we but know what to do with it."

—RALPH WALDO EMERSON

CONTENTS

INTRODUCTION   9

THE GIFTS OF UNCERTAINTY

   I   LEARNING ABOUT UNCERTAINTY   21

   II   RETHINKING UNCERTAINTY   37

   III THE TRUTH ABOUT ADVENTURE   45

   IV THE GIFTS OF ADVENTURE   51

   V   THE HERO'S JOURNEY   61

TAKING A HERO'S JOURNEY

   VI THE DEPARTURE   73

       1 SEE YOUR LIFE AS A HERO'S JOURNEY   77

       2 KNOW THAT THE FIRST STEP
          IS THE HARDEST   81

   VII THE INITIATION   87

       1 DON'T PANIC   89

       2 KEEP MOVING   95

       3 KEEP PERSPECTIVE   99

       4 EMBRACE YOUR FREEDOM   103

5 NAVIGATE, EVALUATE, INNOVATE — *107*

6 SWIM DOWNSTREAM — *111*

7 TRUST THE FORCE — *115*

8 REMEMBER THE NIGHT IS ALWAYS DARKEST RIGHT BEFORE DAWN — *121*

9 LEARN FROM YOUR MISTAKES — *125*

10 SEEK AND NURTURE FRIENDS AND KINDRED SPIRITS — *129*

11 ENJOY THE VIEW — *135*

VIII THE RETURN — *137*

1 TAKE NOTES AND REFLECT — *141*

2 REMEMBER THAT GROWTH HAPPENS SLOWLY — *149*

3 APPLY WHAT YOU'VE LEARNED — *155*

CONCLUSION — *157*

ABOUT THE AUTHOR — *163*

INTRODUCTION

The first thing that hits me is the silence. Silence as profound and unbroken as the field of ice and snow stretching out in front of me, 11,000 feet up in the French Alps. The jagged rock peaks of Petite and Grand Fourche jut up sharply behind me, and it's chilly in the shadows of the early morning air. I look around from my precarious foothold on the steep slope of rough glacial ice, and a second thought begins to sink in. I am completely and utterly alone. No companions, no distant climbers in sight, no other humans or mammals as far as the eye can see. Just ice, snow, and jagged rocky pinnacles rimming a frozen expanse of white. I look down, and a third thought registers. I'm wearing tennis shoes. Shorts, a T-shirt, a light fleece jacket … and tennis shoes.

Dear God. How in hell did I get *here*?

Five minutes earlier, I'd been comfortably ensconced in the left seat of a small mountain ski plane, taking some instruction from an expert flight instructor. Since the morning conditions were so nice, he asked if I'd like to try landing on one of the Alpine glaciers high up in the Mont Blanc range. I said sure. We circled over the landing site, checked the winds, and came around to land. The plan was to land uphill, turn 180 degrees, and take off again downhill.

But in the shadows of Grand Fourche, the icy snow gripped more tightly than I expected. We began the turn, but the skis got stuck in the snow halfway through the turn. After a couple of unsuccessful attempts to free the plane from the ice, the instructor leaned over and opened up my half of the canopy. "I need your help," he yelled over the noise of the running engine. "Go to the wingtip and push back as I add full power. That should rotate us. But once the plane turns, I don't have brakes, so I'm going to have to take off. Make your way down to the tracks down there …" He gestured to some tracks further down the glacier, where the slope was shallower and the snow was in the sun. "… and I'll come back and pick you up there."

I *did* think to grab a fleece jacket as I nodded and climbed out of the plane. But focused on the needs of the mission, I didn't take anything else. I climbed gingerly off the plane's low wing and made my way carefully around the down-slope wing until I was at the front edge of the wingtip. The ice was thick this morning, I noted as I kicked two toe-holds through the crusty surface to give me some traction to push against.

I leaned into the wing as the instructor ran up the engine and the plane started to shift. I ducked under the wing as it pivoted sharply toward me, turning in time to see the plane lifting off and heading out toward the lower end of the glacier.

I watched the red and white ski plane get small in the distance, the sound of its retreating engine quickly swallowed by the vast, uninhabited silence of the glacier and its surrounding mountain peaks. And there I was.

Standing in the midst of all that majestic snow, rock and ice.

Alone.

It all seemed vaguely amusing until I took my first step downhill. My foot shot out from under me on the slick ice and I very nearly fell. And falling a long distance across such rough ice in shorts ... I cringed as I envisioned the shredded skin, blood, friction burns and pain. My heart started pounding. This was actually quite serious. And I didn't have a clear vision as to how I was going to make it come out okay—even without the added challenge of what I might be facing if the pilot and plane *didn't* come back to get me.

While the drama of an icy glacier high in the French Alps may make this story particularly gripping, the emotions that ran through me as I surveyed the seriousness and uncertainty of my situation that morning would be very familiar to anyone who's found themselves on unexpectedly shaky ground, with no clear map or guide to tell them where to go next or how to safely get there. It's what every adventurer feels when exciting plans morph into uncertain and risky reality. It's what every entrepreneur feels when they finally sever their ties to their previous career, and it's what every successfully employed person feels when they're told that the company is closing its doors or their job has been eliminated or outsourced.

Uncertainty is inherently stressful and uncomfortable. When I was a kid, I'd sometimes skip ahead to the end of a book to reassure myself about how it all turned out so I could enjoy the uncertainty of the hero's fate along the way. But when we have to live that uncertainty in real-time, there's not a lot of comfort available to us. Especially if we didn't choose or plan to put ourselves in a situation where the outcome was so unknown ... or *unknowable*.

But here's an important reality check. Certainty is an illusion. Just ask anyone who's ever unexpectedly lost a job or gotten one of those dreaded family emergency phone calls. Life turns on a dime, and the only constant is change. On a very long transcontinental night flight a number of years ago, when I'd gotten a phone call saying there'd been an accident and my father wasn't expected to live the night, I found myself sitting next to a man who was in the same awful boat that I was. I'd bought the only available seat on the next flight to New York, which happened to be in first class. My seat-mate traveled first class as a matter of course. But he'd been camping with his two sons in California when his only sister had been in a terrible car accident. By the time his family got word to him, she'd died. All his wealth hadn't managed to protect him from the loss, or even get him home soon enough to say good-bye.

Life is uncertain, no matter how successful we are or how much money we have. So what do we do about that? If we're smart, we dig our heels in a little less firmly and learn to work with uncertainty, instead of simply trying to ward it off. Because somewhere underneath all the discomfort and stress that comes with it, uncertain times and situations actually contain some valuable lessons, gifts, and opportunities.

Take my predicament on the French glacier. I may have found myself dressed in appallingly inappropriate clothing, on a hazardous slope, with no clear or safe route between point A, where I was, and point B, where I could be rescued. But I had a secret weapon at my disposal:

I am no stranger to uncharted landscapes. Somewhere long ago, I found peace with the uncertainty of my life's path and all the planned and unplanned adventures it entailed. So while I didn't know exactly how to cope with traversing a rough and slippery glacial slope in tennis shoes, I knew what steps I had to take to figure it out.

One. Focus. Falling is not an option, so balance is key and each step has to be very sure. Two. Prioritize. How do I MAKE each step very sure? This answer is very important. Three. Experiment. Kick a heel-hold in the ice. That works. Step firmly. Yes, I can make that hold. Kick another step. Whoa! Too far!!! Note to self: To keep center of gravity and balance, steps must be very small. Four. Remember to breathe. Don't panic. Ask self: "Are you okay *right now*?" Yes. Okay. This can work. Five. Keep perspective. One step at a time. Don't get overwhelmed by the distance to be covered. Take it one step at a time. Six. Take another step. WHOA! Okay, going straight downhill is too steep to manage. Back to three. Experiment. Try cutting diagonally across the slope. Four. Breathe. Five. Keep perspective. Stop, catch your breath, and remember to look around. When are you likely to find yourself alone on a glacier again? Wow. These peaks are staggeringly beautiful. Let me not forget that this isn't just stressful. It's also magical, beautiful, and vividly breathtaking. Be present. Be alive, and be thankful. Funny how that calms the heart. Okay. Back to one. Focus. Two. Step. Four. Breathe. Five. Repeat.

It took longer than I ever would have imagined, but I eventually made my way down safely to the flatter portion of the glacier, where the ski plane awaited me. All ended well. And for all the stress and uncertainty that morning entailed, I now have a sense of how profound silence can be, and a memory of a stark but breathtakingly unspoiled landscape burned indelibly into my mind.

All of which is to say … coping with uncertainty is never comfortable or easy. But learning to deal with it can make future encounters less overwhelming. And that, in turn, not only makes uncertainty easier to cope with, and gives you far more ability to succeed in the face of it … it also frees up enough brain space to allow you to see some of the unexpected gifts that might be traveling in its pockets.

So. How do you come to terms with uncertainty? First and foremost, you stop looking at it as something evil and awful that should be avoided at all cost. Because uncertainty can actually be a wonderful gift. Don't believe me? Keep reading.

THE GIFTS OF UNCERTAINTY

I

LEARNING ABOUT UNCERTAINTY

When I was a teenager, my worst nightmare about my future was that I would somehow fall into the horrifying "rut" I'd heard so many adults complain about, where nice, safe, and completely predictable days would blur into a one long repetitious routine, and I'd wake up at 65 or 70, not quite sure where it all went. I didn't know exactly what I wanted to do with my life, but I knew what I *didn't* want. So when I read that the phrase "May you live in interesting times" was considered a curse in ancient China, it made no sense to me. I *wanted* an interesting and changing life!

Yes. Well. As the saying goes, be very careful what you wish for.

Driven by my desire for adventure and a more interesting life—and my terror of falling into a pre-programmed rut if I didn't take positive action to prevent it—I left college after two years and took off for New Zealand. I didn't intend to live there forever, but I planned to stay long enough to have some adventures and, ostensibly, figure out if I even *wanted* to come home and finish college, or just keep traveling.

Why New Zealand? In part, because it was so far away. But also because everything I read about it painted a picture of a remote and rugged island country that was enticingly adventurous and exotic; the antithesis of the Ivy League environment I was leaving.

New Zealand is, in fact, a small and provincial country known predominantly for its rugby, sailing, sheep and native Maori culture. It's small enough that in some places, its width can be traversed in only three hours by car. But in the span of its two narrow islands, it gathers in almost all variations of natural splendor and challenge, from tropical beaches to glacier-covered alps and fiord-

lands. Even after more than 200 years of European set-
tlement, the land is still more wild than tame, with cities
and towns separated by large stretches of coastal cliffs,
rolling, emerald hillsides, and dramatic volcanic peaks.
When I lived there, New Zealand was also populated by
a scant three million people against 20 million sheep.

Today, New Zealand is known as a vacation adventurer's playground. But in 1981, it was still closer to a
frontier land. Many houses had no central heating, and
the only clothes washer at my disposal was a portable
tub design with a hand-wringer on top. A lot of the
phones were museum pieces with heavy handsets and
rotary dials, and some of the offices still used manual
typewriters. What's more, the laws prohibiting women
from entering public bars had only been rescinded a few
years earlier.

It was not a culture that welcomed foreigners or
immigrants—a fact that might have given me pause, had
I been a little more versed in the challenges of the world.
But it was certainly a far cry from New York. Which, as
far as I was concerned, was selling point enough. I landed
in the city of Auckland on a cold winter day, half a world

away from home, with no friends, no contacts, no job, and a grand total of $500 in my pocket. I wasn't even 20 years old.

The good news about putting yourself in that kind of situation is that you don't have to agonize overmuch about what to do next. Necessity dictates everything. Shelter, food, employment. In that order. And there *is* a kind of refreshing clarity in focusing on the simple basics of survival, whether it's on a rocky mountainside or as a new arrival in a distant land and culture. The demons of loneliness and fear don't set in until or unless you have a little more time and bandwidth available.

Restless and unclear of what, exactly, I was looking for, I spent the next six months as an itinerant worker, taking jobs ranging from selling advertising space and temp work as a legal secretary to a stint working in a corrugated cardboard factory. I made ends meet, but the unsettled nature of my work and life made every day an adventure in unpredictability.

I was friendly with some people. But close friendships, even with people interested in making that kind of connection, take time to develop. So I spent a lot of time alone, both in the cities and on a long backpacking trip I took in the mountains of the South Island. At one point while I was hiking, I went over a week without seeing another human, and the only mammal I encountered was a stray mountain goat that bounded quickly across my path.

But without the distraction of human company, I also had a lot of time to think, observe, and absorb my surroundings. And on that solitary backpacking trip, I experienced the single most beautiful vista I have ever seen, despite all the world travel I've done since then. Several days into my trek, I crested a coastal ridge on the north end of the South Island and found myself face to face with a panorama so astoundingly beautiful that it literally took my breath away. Immediately in front of me was an emerald green mountain slope, dense with waterfalls and tropical foliage, cascading down to a perfect, uninhabited white crescent beach. The beach curved around to a rocky point, cradling South Pacific waters whose colors blended seamlessly from pale turquoise at the sand's edge to an eye-watering cobalt blue further out toward the shimmering horizon.

I didn't articulate the thought at the time, but in that moment I learned one of the many important truths about life and adventure: that there are, as a friend of mine likes to say, some experiences that are only available to those who are willing to have them.

After the backpacking trip, I headed north and got a job working on a farm in one of the valleys east of Auckland. So if I ever need to make a fast escape using a manual-transmission tractor, I now possess the skills to pull it off. I lived with a neighboring farm family for those last couple of months—and, in the process, developed my first real friendships of the journey.

As the six month mark of my stay approached, however, I decided to head home again. In the course of all my travels and adventures, I'd learned I could take care of myself and figure out survivable solutions, even in some tough situations. But I'd also learned how lonely the life of an itinerant explorer could be; how easily world traveling could become as much of a rut as staying in one place. I'd also figured out a compelling reason to return home and finish my degree: so no matter where my life went after that, I'd have other options besides working in a corrugated cardboard factory. It's amazing how clear a little perspective can make things, sometimes.

It had been an interesting and challenging time; full of uncertainty and learning and new experiences. But as I packed my bags on the farm for my flight back to the States, I thought I was on the home stretch of the adventure.

In truth, the real adventure was just beginning. And any remaining ideas about certainty or safety were about to leave my life forever.

Because I'd formed such good friendships with the family I lived with on the farm, all five of them—the parents, and two sons and a daughter around my age—piled into the boys' souped-up 1968 Fairmont sedan to take me to the airport. I sat in the middle of the front seat, with the two boys on either side of me.

The center seat in the Fairmont had no seat belt, and the driver and passenger belts were the old, set-length type, with detachable shoulder harnesses. New Zealand had a seat belt law, even back in 1981, but—as far as I could tell—few people obeyed it. Nevertheless, when John, in the passenger seat, saw a police car coming toward us on the country highway, he reached over and draped his seat belt and shoulder harness across his chest, so it would look as if he were wearing it.

"Oh, please," I scoffed. "If you're going to go to that much trouble, you might as well plug the darn thing in, so it'll actually do you some good." John rolled his eyes but plugged in the seat belt.

Less than two minutes later, our world exploded.

I never even saw the car approaching from the intersecting side road—undoubtedly because it had been going 90 mph, driven by a drunk and angry young man who'd just lost his job. It was just suddenly there, in front of us. There was no time to brake, scream, or react. We simply slammed into it full-speed. And without a seat belt to hold me back, my head went through the front windshield, taking out the rear-view mirror along the way.

John apparently caught a glimpse of the car as it approached from his side and grabbed hold of me, which is why I'm still here to tell the tale. Even with his strong, burly arms, he couldn't hold me back. But he slowed my forward progress enough, injuring both shoulders in the process, that my body didn't leave the car.

Nonetheless, my injuries were still dire. The other car flipped up and over in the air, landing on its roof. We didn't flip, but we spun around twice before thudding to a halt. And when all the movement stopped, John discovered that my head had been split open to the bone from just above my eye to more than halfway back along my skull, with a gap of missing flesh where the mirror had hit.

Odd as it might sound, your body knows, even before your brain can fully process it, when an injury is potentially mortal. Nobody had to tell me. I knew. John pulled me out of the wreckage and laid me down on the side of the road, trying desperately to hold my head together and staunch the bleeding. And I began what would turn out to be a nine-hour, highly focused fight for consciousness and my life—and a much longer struggle for full physical and emotional recovery.

One of the many surreal realizations I had, in the interminable wait for help and treatment following the crash, is just how easy death is. Fighting against it isn't an instinct, when you're that badly injured. It's a choice. And it's not the easy choice.

Slowly, as we waited for help beside the road, the noise and sensations around me all began to seem very far away, as if I were listening to voices in an unseen play from a distant and uncaring vantage point in the dark. And as it all drifted further away, the realization dawned on me that all I had to do was let go, and it would all stop. Death was just that easy. Like letting go of the monkey bars and falling softly into the leaves below.

But in that moment of choice, when death was easy and life was going to be a hard, painful, and possibly unsuccessful fight ... I decided, in a burst of anger and fierce determination, that I wasn't going. I wasn't *done* yet. Life might be hard, uncertain and painful, but it was also full of beauty, love, and joy. And those parts of life, suddenly all the more precious because of their impending loss, were more than worth the trade. Death wasn't going to take all that away from me without a fight.

Slowly, painfully, I clawed my way back to full consciousness on the side of the road. "Don't let me go to sleep," I told John. "Keep me talking. If I don't stay awake, I don't think I'll make it through this." And he did. He stayed with me through the nine hours of agonizing waiting for treatment, through a nightmare surgery, and for the next three days, until I was finally out of the woods.

Eventually I recovered, with few lasting side-effects. The scars are hard to even see today. But I emerged on the far side of that time with my understanding and perspective on life fundamentally and permanently altered.

For one thing, any thoughts I might have had about life being safe, certain, or lasting any particular length of time were gone. We all might know, intellectually, that life is uncertain, that accidents happen, and that we're not guaranteed any particular span of years. But for the most part, we don't internalize that knowledge on a gut, visceral level. Sure, accidents happen, but we don't truly believe they're going to happen *to us*. That's part of what allows us to venture out every morning into the risky world beyond our doors.

But it *had* happened to me. Out of nowhere. I wasn't doing anything risky, just driving to the airport. And I'd come within a hair's breadth of dying. Even more disturbing was the seemingly thin sliver of circumstances that had saved me. I owed my life to another human's actions … and perhaps to an offhand comment I'd made about a seat belt, prompted by a chance passing of a police car. For if John hadn't been strapped in, he couldn't have helped me. We both, most likely, would have died.

So what do you do with such unsettling realizations of chance, risk and fate? I'm sure the answer differs greatly, from one person to the next. But in my case, I eventually came to two conclusions. The first was a fundamental acceptance of life's inherent uncertainty. The accident took away some innocence and a level of comfort I might otherwise have had, especially at the young age of 20. But if you recognize and accept the uncertainty of life on a deep, emotional and visceral level, then all the things in it become far more precious. And that was my second conclusion. I might not be able to control how long I lived, but I could certainly control how *well* I spent the time I had.

Other people might tolerate a career in an unfulfilling job in the hopes of a comfortable retirement. But without the confidence that I'd necessarily live that long, that kind of trade-off wasn't one I could make. I didn't become reckless about the future, but quality of life in the present became far more important to me. In addition, once you've been to the edge of life and back, the trappings of money, status and "things" becomes less important. Those were not the parts of life that, in that moment on the edge, had inspired me to fight so hard to survive.

What *was* worth fighting for … what really *mattered* … was very clear to me. People mattered. Experiencing and understanding as much of the world as I could mattered. Quality and authenticity mattered. Grabbing hold of life with two hands and taking the ride for all it was worth, regardless of how long the ride lasted … mattered.

My life didn't change right away. I finished my degree and even spent the first five years out of college pursuing a conventional corporate career. But in the end, I think that sense of urgency about living fully in the present is what gave me the courage to pitch that successful marketing career, with all the income, security, and comfort it provided, in search of a more fulfilling life path.

Being a writer might not pay as well as a corporate marketing job. And it certainly wasn't the easiest career track I could have chosen. But it offered me the chance to explore the world, experience a wide variety of sights, sensations, people and places, and create something valuable from my heart by writing about what I saw, learned, and experienced along the way.

The flying came as a bit of a coincidental after-thought; the unexpected result of a simple idea that it would be fun to get a ride in an old, open-cockpit biplane. It's a long story that starts with the fact that the guys with the airplane weren't licensed to sell rides, so I had to work on the plane for a day to earn my flight ... and discovered, in the process, that working on airplanes was kind of fun. One thing led to another, and I was soon trading work on the planes for flying lessons.

But the truth is, I pursued my pilot's license because flying had a way of focusing me completely on each moment of living, as it happened. Yes, the activity entailed risk. But it also opened up a whole new world of adventures, places, and experiences and made me feel completely and totally alive. The trade-offs, to my way of thinking, were well worth it.

That was 25 years ago. In the years since, my adventures have taken me to six continents and from 120 feet below sea level to 70,000 feet above the Earth. My income has fluctuated in lurches and dives, and figuring out how to stay solvent is sometimes as great a challenge as any physical adventure I've undertaken. My life is, in many ways, a study in uncertainty. But it's also full to overflowing with learning, wonder, possibility and joy. And yes, there is a link.

In some ways, it would have been nice to have a crystal ball to provide reassurance that it would all work out okay. Or so much cushion, financially and emotionally, that not knowing how any next bit of life was going to go would have been a little less stressful. But if I am a far wiser and stronger person than I was 25 years ago, it's precisely because I didn't have that crystal ball or margin.

Emotional strength, it turns out, is something we all have to build for ourselves. Just like physical strength, there's no shortcut, best-seller, or magical piece of parental or coaching advice that can confer it on us easily, without a lot of sweat and effort. And living with uncertainty offers a daily dose of strength training.

There are times when the challenges feel overwhelming, even now. But live with anything long enough—kids, illness, physical adversity or uncertainty—and it begins to feel almost normal. That's the great part about human nature. We can adapt to an astounding range of life circumstances, if we have to. And as we adapt, we begin to see things we never noticed before. It's like stepping out of a well-lit house into the shadows of a moonless night. At first, all you can see is the dark. But if you open yourself to the shadows, instead of trying to keep them at bay with a protective flashlight, your eyes eventually adjust—and can reveal a dazzling array of stars.

II

RETHINKING UNCERTAINTY

Few people are ever granted what they wish for in their youth, so I consider myself extremely fortunate, in that regard. I've gotten to explore reaches of the planet that few people ever see. And whatever else I might say about my life, it has certainly been interesting.

But looking back on it, I also understand that Chinese curse a lot better. Because for something to be interesting, the outcome has to be somewhat in doubt. It's the reality-check I give myself whenever I'm tempted to complain about my life. Interesting and predictable are inversely proportionate, when it comes to life paths—or even life stories. Think about a reading a book or watching a movie whose ending you already know. Not nearly as interesting as a story where you don't know how or if the hero survives.

Interesting times, in other words, are almost always uncertain times. Changing times. And few things in life are as uncomfortable as uncertainty or change. Hence the curse.

On the other hand, Chinese philosophy also includes the concept of yin and yang; opposing forces that exist in tandem with each other. So from that perspective, even a curse must contain within it an equal force for good.

I wouldn't wish the uncertainty of a near-fatal car crash on anybody. But by the same token … without *any* uncertainty, life would lose any possibility for new joys or experiences. We'd become trapped in a *Groundhog Day* nightmare, where life was totally predictable … and utterly unbearable. In the movie by that name, Bill Murray finds himself condemned to live one day over and over again, and ends up trying to commit suicide to avoid the agony of a future where nothing changes. We *need* some amount of change and uncertainty in our lives—not just to avoid having our days descend into a sense-deadening rut, but to keep from going crazy.

But there's more to it than that. While we rarely welcome unplanned detours in our lives, change can be a great source of energy, once we embrace it. Each January 1st, we all enthusiastically plan any number of changes we want to make in the new year. It can take a lot of effort to let go of the past; of all that was known and comfortable. But it also feels good to start a new chapter, with new possibilities. I have a friend, in fact, who says she loves moving, because it gives her a chance to shed stuff she doesn't need anymore, redecorate, reinvent, and get a new look and perspective on herself and her life. I can't quite summon her enthusiasm for all the packing and unpacking involved. But she's right. Change *can* be energizing.

Think, for a moment, about the periodic table of elements. The periodic table contains both noble (inert) gases and more active gases. The inert gases, like helium, are nice and predictable and stable, but they don't combine easily with anything else, or create anything particularly interesting. The more active ones, on the other hand … ahhh. Those are the exciting ones. Combine a couple of those, and *huge* amounts of energy can be released.

Mix hydrogen and oxygen and ... well, the *Hindenburg* comes to mind. But all across the periodic table, the actions and mixing of active gases makes amazing new compounds possible. Sparks. Fire. Transformation. Whole new worlds!

So uncertainty leads to change, and change releases energy. Even if it's not always a smooth or gentle process.

But energy isn't the only compelling reason or reward for learning how to cope with change. Consider the lessons of evolution. The species that survive are those that learn to adapt well to changing external circumstances or pressures. The ancient Dodo bird might have been a lovely animal. But scientists believe that it found such abundant food on the island of Mauritius that it gradually lost its ability to fly. Too much comfort and security, you might say. That was fine, except then the world changed. Humans arrived and depleted the forests that provided the Dodo's food sources, and the Dodo couldn't adapt its diet or ability to move fast enough. And so it became extinct.

If humans have survived thus far, it's been because we proved ourselves better at adapting to a changing world. In fact, many anthropologists believe it was only when our ancient ancestors were forced to leave the safety of the trees and descend into the less-secure grasslands that they began to develop the skills and features that would differentiate them from other animals. Which is to say, the best way to get good at anything is to have some practice at it. Ironically, we humans still often resist the discomfort of change—even though our survival depends on getting good at handling it—until outside circumstances force us to change, or the pain of *not* changing becomes even more uncomfortable. But the fact remains: embracing uncertainty and change, instead of trying to stave them off, strengthens our ability to survive big and unstoppable changes and challenges that come at us from the outside.

"Yes, but a little uncertainty goes a long way," one might answer. True. And sometimes life throws us an overload of uncertainty that shifts the balance from "exciting" to "scary." After all, there is a fine line between those two—both in movies and in real life. When there's a bit of unpredictability about what's going to happen within a house, that helps keep life interesting. When the entire house starts to crumble around us, that generally tilts the balance into no-kidding scary.

Four years after I'd pitched the safety of my corporate

career to become a writer and a pilot, I split up with the man I'd been living with for eight years. I was suddenly not just self-employed, but *sole-income*-self-employed. And my entire life as I'd known or planned it—house, yard, airplane, comfortable circle of friends—abruptly disappeared. Looking back on that time honestly, I also can't say I felt particularly energized by all that change. I felt as if I'd been thrown onto the outer reaches of a weak tree limb over a cold and raging river, bereft of any security or comfort and battered by the harsh winds of the world.

But my mother, who had a few more years' life experience under her belt, saw it differently. "Lane, you have an amazing opportunity here," I remember her telling me. "Most people only get one time in their life, when they leave high school or college, when they get to reinvent themselves and their lives—to be anything and go anywhere, with no ties to stop them. You're being given a second chance to do that, with all the extra knowledge you've gained in the years in between. *Embrace* your freedom. Make good use of it! Who knows if or when you'll get this chance again!"

Now, of course, I can see she was right. The truth is,

few times in our lives hold more possibility, or greater chances for discovery and reward, than times when the solid walls and routines that structured and held us crumble. Whether we leave by choice, or are thrown there by circumstance, that crumbling gives us the rare opportunity to build a new house or chart a new life course, in any colors, shape, or direction we want. It also gives us an opportunity to discover strengths we never knew we had and teaches us valuable lessons about ourselves, life, and the world.

This is not to say building that new house or charting that new direction will be entirely fun, or as comfortable as staying in the old house—as anyone who's ever undertaken the construction of a new house can attest. So why do we put up with the hassle, discomfort and inconvenience of building a new house? Sometimes we have no choice. But if we undertake the effort voluntarily, it's because we realize that the new house, once it's built, will be much better than the last. And if we choose the extra trouble of a custom-built home, we can end up with an environment that will suit us far better in the long run than anything the easier, ready-built models offer.

If all that isn't enough reason to reconsider the evils of uncertainty, think about this: uncertainty is a prerequisite for adventure. In fact, it's a defining component. I've often said to my friends that if you know how something's going to turn out, it's a vacation, not an adventure. The corollary to this, of course, is that when a vacation goes so wrong as to become an unpredictable Chevy Chase movie plot, it has ceased to be a vacation and has instead morphed *into* an adventure.

So if or when life suddenly veers into unpredictable and slightly scary territory, regardless of whether it's by choice or circumstance, or whether it's in terms of a job, an economy, your personal life, or being stranded on an icy glacier … all it really means is that life has launched you on an adventure. With or without your permission. And while that may feel less than comfortable, it's not all bad. In fact, it can be one of the best things that's ever happened to you. For if my life has taught me nothing else, it's taught me that the gifts of adventure are plentiful, precious … and utterly unattainable in the safety of an unchanging life or living room.

III

THE TRUTH ABOUT ADVENTURE

Most of us dream about adventure when we're young. We read stories of great explorers whose lives sound far more exciting than our own, and we dream of sailing or flying or climbing our way to exotic places and experiences. But all those notions of adventure tend to be more than a little rose-tinted.

Back before I went to New Zealand, survived a car accident, or learned how to fly, I remember reading the stories of Antoine de St. Exupéry (the author of *The Little Prince*) who flew the mail in South America and Africa in the 1930s. And I remember thinking how wonderful his adventures sounded. He spoke of spending desert nights across from steely-eyed, saber-armed Moors in northern Africa, and of the heightened sensations the danger awakened in him and in his companions, who were soldiers in the French Foreign Legion. I pictured a group of men sitting around a small fire on a warm desert night in an exotic and distant land, looking up at a dazzling array of stars overhead, and I felt a stab of envy. Suburban New York wasn't nearly so interesting.

But then, not too long ago, I found myself climbing out of a small airplane in the desert of eastern Chad. The one small building at the old airport was a crumbling concrete structure, and an outpost of the French Foreign Legion was still stationed at the far end of the runway. The sabers had been replaced with AK-47s, but aside from that, the turban-wrapped warriors swarming around the airport could have been straight out of one of St. Ex's books. Many were dressed in long, flowing djellabahs, with long strips of turban fabric wrapped around their lower faces to protect against the desert sand and wind. The only exposed part of their faces was their eyes—which conveyed no human connection, warmth, or inclination to mercy. Steely, indeed. Suddenly, all those exciting desert nights I'd read about took on a decidedly darker tinge, and suburban New York began to seem a whole lot more appealing. It's funny, how different adventure feels when its hazards and consequences are real and there's no guarantee the story has a happy ending.

In fact, standing there on the crumbling tarmac in Abeche, Chad, it struck me that St. Ex probably felt the exact same way when he was actually facing all those cyclones, sandstorms, and steely-eyed warriors who'd just as soon kill him as look at him. Because few adventures feel as great while you're in the middle of them as they sound when you're planning them ahead of time, or when you talk or write about them after the fact. In part, this is because if you're coping with challenging and uncertain circumstances, you're focused on immediate tasks and needs. Unless you specifically remind yourself to stop, breathe, and look around while you're busy with those other things, you often don't have a lot of spare brain space to think about how beautiful or exotic or cool it is. You're just trying to make sure you come through it okay.

But it's also because adventure rarely, if ever, happens

in a comfort zone. Generally speaking, if you're in the middle of a full-blown, real-life adventure, you're not dwelling on how much fun you're having. You're wondering what *possessed* you to think this was a good idea. Or how to kill the person who caused this situation to occur. No kidding. In all the adventures I've had over the years, whether it was climbing or flying through mountains, wreck diving in the South Pacific, flying into conflict zones or jungles, venturing solo across continents or into foreign countries, starting my own business, or leaving unhappy jobs or relationships—all experiences I also wouldn't trade for the world, mind you—every single one contained at least one moment where I knew I'd make a huge mistake, and I wished I were somewhere else. It comes with the territory.

The odd thing is, this truth seems to hold regardless of whether the adventure is great or small, physical, financial, professional, or personal. Because while we tend to think of adventure in terms of grand, physical challenges like climbing Mt. Everest, or Indiana Jones-type explorations into exotic lands and cultures ... the truth is, adventure can be found anywhere. It can be found in attempting a new skill, or moving to an unfamiliar place. It can be found in starting a business, pursuing a life's dream, or even figuring out how to pay the rent after an unexpected job loss. It can be found in rejecting a secure paycheck that offers everything but fulfillment, or in leaving a comfortable relationship that contains everything but love. Adventure, in short, is what happens anytime any of us step out of routine and comfort into a place where our footing is a little uncertain, the outcome is a little unpredictable, *but*—and this part is important—the possibilities are suddenly wide open.

The power of adventure is that when the maps and guides disappear, we both have to, and learn that we *can*, find our own path through the wilderness. And while trailblazing isn't always comfortable, it's a creative process that can be empowering, educational, energizing ... and full of unexpected gifts and joy.

IV

THE GIFTS OF ADVENTURE

In June of 2000, I decided to fly my own airplane—solo—across the United States, from southern California to Key West, Florida. Important to note, here, is that my airplane is a relatively basic machine that sometimes goes slower than the cars on the roads below, if the headwinds are strong enough. It has trouble climbing above 8,000 feet on a hot summer day, and it also doesn't have a lot of electronic equipment, maps, or automatic systems in it. So flying across a continent was guaranteed to be a multi-day adventure with more than a few terrain, weather and navigational challenges. And that was if nothing else broke or went wrong. The good news was, I didn't have to follow one particular road, or even a particular speed limit. I had the expanse of an entire continent and sky in front of me, and almost unlimited freedom in terms of how I chose to traverse and explore it. But the cost of that freedom was that I was going to have to figure out each and every mile of the way by myself.

From the moment my wheels left the ground in California, I left all certainty and comfort behind. I'd never flown the route before, so I had no idea what to expect. I had a route planned, but I also knew that in flying, as in life, even the best-laid plans are subject to change, at all times. I would most likely have to innovate and adjust that plan many times along the way.

And yet, uncertain paths have their advantages, as well. While known routes may be easier and more comfortable to follow, comfort and routine can become dangerous sedatives that lull us into walking through our lives only half awake, or half alive. One of the great gifts of adventure is that it jolts us fully alive again, waking up senses we'd all but forgotten about.

One of the reasons that awakening happens is because our survival genes kick in when the going gets uncertain, sharpening our senses so we can detect danger better and find the best way forward. If we remember best those moments of uncertain adventure and drama in our lives, it's partly because our senses were taking it all in with extra care and precision.

But there's more to it than that. When the path forward suddenly becomes murky, we also have to pay more attention to where we put each step. As a result, we become more *aware* of each step; each choice and moment as it happens. And that simple process of refocusing our attention on the present, instead of the future or the past, can profoundly affect what we see and how we feel.

On the last leg of my cross-country flight, from Fort Lauderdale to Key West, Florida, the air traffic controllers said they needed me to stay a mile offshore and within 500 feet of the water so I wouldn't interfere with traffic departing the coastal airports. Even though the weather was clear and beautiful, flying that low is demanding. There isn't a lot of room or time to correct a problem or mistake at 300 or 400 feet. So you have to stay very focused on your actions and surroundings. But *because* I was so focused, I also noticed many subtle but wonderful details about my world as I flew along.

I watched seagulls and water birds taking off beneath me, leaving delicate trails in the water behind them as they gathered speed for takeoff. And the water itself, I realized, was far from a simple shade of ocean blue. It was a sparkling, transparent montage of blues and greens, clear enough that I could see all the way to the bottom of the sandy ocean shallows. And across that underwater landscape were rippling sand dunes, islands of submerged plant life, and dark green channels of deeper water streaming out from the shores of the nearby Keys.

My focus on the details surrounding me in that moment also wiped all the other clutter out of my mind. All that remained were my impressions of the world around me and the few really critical pieces of information I needed to figure out my next steps safely ... my airspeed, my altitude, my location and heading, and a quick check to make sure all the engine instruments were happy. And in the space that simpler focus allowed, I remembered again just how beautiful and diverse a place the world is, and how many possibilities it holds. As that thought registered, I also felt a surge of excitement about what that possibility-filled world might still have to offer me. Amazing, what a little perspective can do for the soul.

I felt something else, as well, flying low over the water with no thoughts except for what I was experiencing, right then and there. I felt *alive*. For, as a friend once said to me, "the secret to feeling 100% alive isn't to live for the moment, but to live as if to make each moment last forever." It's why three-year-olds, so completely immersed in the glee of a spontaneous bout of laughter, seem so much more vividly alive than the rest of us. And it's a big part of why adventure, for all its discomfort, is so invigorating. The uncertainty of adventure requires us to focus our complete attention on each moment, as we live it. And completely immersed in that moment, we regain the ability feel all the life it holds.

For over an hour, I banked gently a few hundred feet above the Florida Straits, not quite able to stand the beauty and wonder of it all without laughing out loud with joy. I might even have given a three-year-old a run for their money, on that front. And those images are almost as vivid in my mind now, 10 years later, as they were when I landed in Key West.

I don't know how long I will end up living. But I know that I will have spent more of my life awake, and fully alive, because of the more adventurous paths I've followed.

I've also learned that even the harder parts of adventure have their gifts—because navigating uncertainty is nothing if not educational. Faced with unpredictable challenges, you develop new skills and expand your knowledge about the world. Each time you take on the unknown, there's less "unknown" territory left to intimidate you. Working your way through an uncertain landscape also forces you to face your strengths, weaknesses, hopes and fears in a way that no routine, well-marked road ever will.

On one particularly memorable leg of my flight to Key West, a controller in Pensacola, Florida diverted me three miles out over the Gulf of Mexico, where the visibility and clouds were much lower than they were along the shoreline. I had to keep descending to stay clear of the clouds, and I was soon only 600 feet above the waves. I could still see the coast. But if things got any worse, I might easily lose that reference point. I asked to come back closer to shore, but the controller denied me permission, saying he had other traffic along the shoreline.

As I contemplated my options, I felt waves of fear rising up within me. This wasn't good. The weather was deteriorating, and the danger I was facing was real. But when I took a deep breath and asked myself, "Are you okay *right now*?" the answer, surprisingly, was "yes." I was in a perfectly sound airplane, with wings level, engine purring contentedly, and I could still see both the shoreline and the water beneath me. I was not about to crash. I was just afraid that the conditions would worsen so much that those things might not be true a few miles down the road.

I was afraid, in other words, of what *might* happen in the future, not what was happening to me in that instant. Once I figured that out, I realized that all I needed to do was formulate a plan to keep that scary future from coming to pass. I finally decided that if I couldn't see the shoreline anymore, or if I had to descend below 500 feet, I was going to declare an emergency and fly straight in to Pensacola. If I declared an emergency, no controller could deny me permission to fly to shore or land. I had a way to keep myself safe. And once I had that plan, I felt the fear slide away.

While I have no great desire to relive that hour of my life, it *was* educational. I learned that while fear can be debilitating, and is something we need to learn how to control, it has a weakness that makes it *possible* to control. Because a lot of the time, we're really afraid of what *might* happen to us a few miles or days or years down the road. Not what's happening to us at any given moment. That's valuable information to have, and I now have that tool in my toolbox to combat the uncertainties of whatever the future throws at me.

The trip I took to Key West was neither comfortable nor easy. But I still wouldn't have traded that week for all the money in the world. Those six days gave me one of the richest treasure troves of memories, lessons, and pure vivid life experience of any stretch of days in my life. And while the lessons of adventure might be particularly sharp when the risks and consequences are physical, *any* adventure—big or small, physical, professional or emotional, and even short, one-time events or challenges—holds potential for life, joy, learning and growth.

On the other hand, not all adventures are equal. While adventure can be found anywhere, there are some adventures that have far more profound and life-changing effects. Their beginning can be voluntary or involuntary. But they are the kind of grand adventure all the epic hero tales talk about—internal and external journeys into the unknown that are so transformative that those who undertake them can return with the strength of a Zen Master, a Greek hero or even a Jedi Knight.

These kinds of powerful and life-changing adventures are called epic hero journeys. And they aren't limited to ancient myths and fictional stories. Real-life people undertake them every day. In fact, if all the security and certainty in your life has suddenly disappeared … you may be in the middle of one, yourself.

"The goal of the journey is to discover yourself."

—JOSEPH CAMPBELL

V

THE HERO'S JOURNEY

Ever since the dawn of civilization, societies have formulated great myths and stories to help guide young people along the path to maturity, strength, and wisdom. The stories present "heroic" role models and describe the rigors of the transformative journey that turn a young man or woman into a greatly respected leader and member of the society.

Unlike the two-dimensional heroes of Disney tales, these epic heroes are everyday people who—either by choice or necessity—leave their comfortable towns or village lives and undertake long, hazardous journeys.

Along the way, they find helpful guides and friends, such as wizards, spirits, or others of great power. They also battle great obstacles and opponents, ranging from towering fortresses and thorny forests to evil wizards and supernatural creatures. And unlike Prince Charming, these epic heroes make a lot of mistakes along the way. They learn as much from their failures as they do from their victories. They doubt. They fear. They struggle through lonely dark nights. They have to learn some hard truths about themselves and the world as they work through an uncertain and scary landscape.

But along the way, these epic heroes also learn about their strengths and what really matters in life. They gain valuable skills and knowledge. They learn *how* to get through dark nights and tough battles. So whether or not they vanquish the evil wizard forever, the heroes emerge strong enough to battle whatever comes at them in the future. They are heroes not because of a sole "heroic" act, or because they are willing to sacrifice themselves for another, but because they are willing to undertake, and stick with, a difficult, uncertain, but transformative journey that brings them face to face with themselves.

And their strength stems from all the knowledge, understanding and wisdom they gain along the way.

Think, for example, about Luke Skywalker in George Lucas's epic hero journey tale, *Star Wars*. When the story begins, Luke is living a very normal, comfortable life on his aunt and uncle's farm. When Obi Wan Kenobi first tries to get him to undertake the journey to save the Rebel Alliance and Princess Leia, Luke turns him down. He *has* a life. But then tragedy hits. The Empire's storm troopers arrive and murder his aunt and uncle, burning down his home. He has no choice anymore. The life he knew has been taken away from him.

Along his journey, Luke encounters friends and aids … Obi Wan, Han Solo, Chewbacca, Yoda, Princess Leia … and terrifying opponents, from storm troopers, Darth Vader and the evil Emperor to any number of hideous monsters. Luke also makes mistakes, including (in Episode V) cutting off his training with Yoda to impetuously jump back into battle—and he pays a price for those mistakes, including his capture and the loss of one of his hands. He endures loss and has to come face to face with some hard truths about himself and his origins. The journey is long, and there are many dark nights of doubt where we're not even sure he's going to survive.

But in the end, he returns and is able to defeat the Death Star—although the Emperor and Darth Vader escape to fight another day—because he has learned enough about himself and the world along the way to *become* a Jedi Knight. He's still human and fallible (as the sequels prove), but he's able to channel his energy, trust and use "The Force," and effectively apply the skills, knowledge and wisdom he acquired by working his way through a life-changing, adventurous and uncertain journey.

Other examples abound, in both classic and popular literature, from Homer's *Odyssey* and Arthurian legends to J.R.R. Tolkien's *Lord of the Rings* and any number of other sci-fi/fantasy genre stories. But all hero journey tales contain certain common elements and themes.

In classic mythology and literature, a hero's journey consists of three stages, and always contains certain defining elements. The three stages of a hero's journey are:

1. The Departure
2. The Initiation
3. The Return

THE DEPARTURE

The hero always starts off as an everyday person, living a normal and generally predictable life. Then something happens to awaken a restlessness in the hero: an invitation or call to adventure. The triggering event may be appealing (the appearance of a friendly, magical wizard) or terrible (the destruction of the hero's village or family). The hero may resist the call for a while, but the hero's journey begins when the hero agrees to leave what he or she knows and embark on an unpredictable journey into the unknown. By crossing that threshold, the hero's life is changed forever. This is the departure.

THE INITIATION

The journey is full of unexpected obstacles, dangers, and trials. The hero must confront inner fears and weaknesses, as well as external challenges and threats. The hero makes mistakes and stumbles along the way, but the experiences teach him or her valuable lessons that add to their strength and wisdom. In addition, while the hero may start alone, once he or she commits to the journey, magical and human guides, friends, and aids appear to help. A hero never triumphs on the strength of their own power alone. This is the initiation.

THE RETURN

Through the rigors of the journey—the triumphs, failures, challenges and misfortunes—the hero gains strength, wisdom, and the ability to move beyond his or her personal limitations and fears. Home and safety are no longer tied to a place or set of circumstances. Home becomes a state of being, and safety lies in the hero's confidence in his or her ability to endure, persevere, and prevail, no matter what the circumstances. And while much of a hero's journey is an internal, personal one of growth, the final stage of the hero's journey occurs when they are able to bring all that newfound strength and wisdom back to their everyday lives, becoming a stronger and more positive force in the world.

This is the Return. And thus is born a true hero.

In literature, of course, the heroes and their challenges are fantastical. Few of us will battle a Death Star, fire-breathing dragons, or shape-shifting wizards. But market forces, problematic bosses, or other challenges we face in real life can *seem* like shape-shifting wizards, sometimes. And that's the point. The hero's journey tale is considered "classic" because, while the details and specific challenges may differ, the growth process the epic hero goes through is something anyone can experience, in one guise or another, in the course of their lives. That's why these tales are so enduring and popular, as well as so useful in teaching how to acquire strength that's not dependent on money, position, superior force, or anything that can be taken away.

It would be nice if we could gain that strength without the hard challenges of a hazardous and difficult journey, just as it would be nice if we could lose weight and have an athletic figure without exercising or going to the gym. But life doesn't work that way. To grow and become stronger, we have to be challenged. And to be challenged, we have to work our way through woods where the path isn't already marked, paved, and set up with refreshment stands every 50 feet.

What differentiates a hero's journey from an everyday, garden-variety adventure? I think it's a matter of scope and depth. Spending a weekend kayaking river rapids can be an adventure, and it may offer many gifts of learning and joy. But unless something unusual happens to spark serious internal contemplation and re-evaluation, three days of kayaking probably won't fundamentally change how someone views themselves and the world.

A hero's journey, on the other hand, isn't just mildly educational. It's transformative, because it's as much an internal journey as an external one. A weekend of river kayaking might be an adventure, but kayaking solo from Alaska to Russia along the Aleutian Island chain could be a transformative hero's journey. As could having to make a significant career or relationship change in mid-life, or leaving a secure job to pursue a life's passion or dream. Why? Because a hero's journey involves making your way through a long enough stretch of uncertainty and challenge that it brings you hard up against yourself and forces you to re-examine all the expectations, truths, fears, strengths, flaws, hopes and doubts you find there. The goal of the journey—or at least what makes it so powerful and rewarding—is, as philosopher and writer Joseph Campbell said, "to discover yourself." For once you have that knowledge, you can handle any amount of uncertainty the world or an Evil Empire can throw at you and still stand tall.

The journey to that strength isn't easy—which is why so many epic heroes, including Frodo Baggins and Luke Skywalker, answered the call to the adventure so reluctantly. And the thing about hero journeys is … no matter how many people have taken them before you, each one is unique. Nobody else can tell you how to make your way through it, or which direction you should follow. There are no easy seven-step plans or formulas for success. Because it's what you learn by "sniff-checking" your way through all that uncertainty, on your own, that gives the journey its power.

But that's not to say you can't learn anything from other people's experiences, or from a better understanding of what the journey entails. When I flew my plane through a tricky stretch in the Rocky Mountains the first time, nobody else could tell me exactly how to do it, or how to handle what I found there. But the stories of others who'd flown that pass before me helped me anticipate and recognize at least some of the challenges and pitfalls I might encounter. Forewarned is forearmed, or something like that.

In addition, surviving the uncertainty of either a momentary adventure or a life-changing turn of events can have a lot to do with how you look at it. If you think of it as all bad, it's going to be awful. But if you recognize that uncertainty can lead to adventure, and a life-changing turn of events can be the start of a powerful and rewarding hero's journey, it can make the process far less painful. It can even open your eyes to gifts, joys, opportunities and wonder you might otherwise have missed. Like I said—it's amazing what a little perspective can do for the soul.

Taking a Hero's Journey

VI

THE DEPARTURE

Modern-day hero journeys may not entail magical chalices, fire-breathing dragons, or intricate spells to change the winds—at least, not literally. But any time you willingly step away from what's known and comfortable to chart your own course, or any time life rips what's known and comfortable away from you and forces you to chart a new course ... you have entered the world of a hero's journey. And it will contain all of those elements—just in different guises. The goal is still a golden chalice beyond price, if you seek it with passion and fervor. There will be fire-breathing dragons, even if they look more like difficult clients, cancelled contracts, or a declining bank balance. And finding your way through all that uncertainty and challenge will require the same kind of strength, skill and creativity as a spell-weaver seeking to harness the wind.

But having lived through journeys both chosen and forced, physical and emotional, large and small, I've learned a few things about surviving and benefiting from the process. That knowledge can't guarantee me success on any new venture, or make the challenges go away. But it gives me a few extra tools in my "life skills" toolbox that help me get through whatever shifting winds or storms I face.

So if you're contemplating any kind or size of adventure, or life has suddenly thrown you out of your comfortable village and into the unpredictable wilds of a life-changing hero's journey, here are a few tips and thoughts you might find helpful.

"You enter the forest at the darkest point, where there is no path. Where there is a way or path, it is someone else's path. You are not on your own path. If you are following someone else's way, you are not going to realize your potential."

—JOSEPH CAMPBELL

1

SEE YOUR LIFE AS A HERO'S JOURNEY

Above and beyond anything else ... remember that anytime you find yourself having to chart a new course with little clear guidance as to the best way forward, you are embarking on what will at least be an adventure, and might very well be a hero's journey. And that puts you in the same class as every epic hero in the history of humankind. The journey may not be easy or entirely comfortable, but it will offer you astounding gifts and rewards. And not the least of those rewards is that the strength and wisdom you gain from finding your way through all that unknown territory, adversity and uncertainty will then be yours forever. Assuming, of course, that you keep your eyes and mind open and try to learn a thing or two from the experience.

As my mother once said to me at the end of a particularly challenging adventure … "Once you have climbed a mountain, no hill will ever seem so tall again."

What's more, keep in mind that for each drop of uncertainty they entail, adventures and hero journeys offer an equal proportion of possibility. If there are no paved roads to follow, you have greater freedom to move anywhere you want. If you don't have a steady job anymore, then leaving the security it offered to pursue something more fulfilling isn't such a painful choice to make. If you don't know what tomorrow will bring, chances are very good that you won't find it boring. And if you have to think hard about how you spend that day, because you don't have someone telling you your job tasks each hour, your brain might start developing new creative talents. You also might come up with energizing new ideas about what activities or work you want to do.

"As you go the way of life, you will see a great chasm. Jump. It is not as wide as you think."

—NATIVE AMERICAN PROVERB

2

KNOW THAT THE FIRST STEP IS THE HARDEST

The great Chinese philosopher Lao Tzu famously said, "The journey of a thousand miles begins with a single step." What he neglected to mention was, that first step can be a doozie. There is nothing harder than willingly stepping away from everything that is known and comfortable to take on the discomfort and uncertainty of an adventure or a hero's journey.

The adventures I've undertaken have given me rewards beyond price or words. I have stood silently on the tip of an uninhabited island in Alaska—surrounded by icebergs, glaciers, and woodland streams—and heard a symphony of music comprised entirely of water sounds. I have retraced the steps of 19th century cattle drovers in the Australian Outback, sleeping beneath the stars and finding rusty souvenirs of the old drovers' passing in the sand beneath my horse's feet. I have sailed across the summer Italian countryside in a slow-moving airship, 500 feet above hillside castles and Medieval towns. I've witnessed traumatized human hearts somehow finding love and life again in African refugee camps. I have stood on a peak high in the Himalayas and been reduced to tears by the beauty and power that touched me there.

And yet, the night before I left on every single one of those adventures, I felt a sudden and almost overwhelming reluctance to leave my nice, safe, comfortable home. Standing on the very edge of a cliff and preparing to jump, thoughts of the exciting possibilities that might open up once we take flight pale beside the sobering realization that there's a leap off a very tall cliff involved in the process, as well. That realization opens up a gap in our determination. And through that gap, our inner demons pounce.

A number of years ago, a friend of mine and his wife

spent almost six months kayaking the Pacific Coast from Alaska to Seattle, Washington. It was an extraordinary experience that added much to their lives. But I still recall his description of his wife's plaintive, exhausted and discouraged cry—"Why must we be so *bold*??"—on a particularly challenging day, when they finally dragged their soggy boats and gear up on a cold and wind-beaten island beach.

"Why must we be so bold?"

"What the hell's wrong with me?"

"Why, again, am I doing this?"

"This is never going to work."

"This is irresponsible."

"I'm crazy."

"What if I can't do it? Or I fail?"

"Is it too late to turn back or cancel?"

Talk to anyone who's ever undertaken a serious adventure or life-changing hero's journey, and you'll find they've probably said all that to themselves, and more. Especially the night before they leapt. I suspect it's why Amelia Earhart once said "courage is the price life exacts for granting peace." Leaping off a cliff, even to pursue a life's dream or a far more fulfilling life path, requires courage. But to turn back in fear, once you're realized you want to see what lies beyond that limit, is to forfeit peace in your soul. You'll forever wonder what might have happened … "if." And life's too precious and short to burden it with that kind of restless, doubt-filled regret.

But here's the good news. Once you've jumped, and staying on the cliff is no longer an option, all that goes away. You're then in it, for better or worse, and your focus shifts—at least most of the time—to more practical matters of where to go next and how. There will still be dark nights of doubt, when things aren't going well, when you'll wonder again if this journey was such a good idea. You may question your sanity, your judgment, your ability, and your courage. But not with the same agony that accompanies the temptation and option of staying in your comfortable old life.

The other good news corollary to this is if you've been thrown off the cliff of comfort and security involuntarily—through trauma, divorce, loss of a job, or other unavoidable life change—you get to bypass all that agony. Boom! You're already past the hardest part, which is deciding whether or not to leap. You don't have a choice. You're already in the land of adventure and hero journeys, whether you like it or not. So now, all you have do is figure out where to go next and how.

This may seem like cold comfort. But sometimes, the lure and comfort of what we know is so strong that we stay in mediocre or unhappy places, unable to justify leaping to ourselves or our families if we don't absolutely have to, even if we know we'd be better off if we left. It's why mother birds kick their babies out of the warmth and comfort of the nest if they linger too long. They're actually doing the babies a favor, even if the baby birds don't immediately recognize it as such as they're being pushed over the edge.

It's something to think about, anyway.

VII

THE INITIATION

Once you're launched on an adventure or a hero's journey ... *then* what? How do you get through it, or figure out the best way to go? How do you get the courage to keep going? How do you know if you have crossed the line between faith and stupidity, or perseverance and stubborn blindness? What happens if you fail? What if it doesn't work out okay? Nobody can answer all those questions for you. But here are a few general tips for surviving and thriving in the midst of any life adventure or hero's journey.

"The only thing we have to fear is fear itself."

—FRANKLIN DELANO ROOSEVELT

1

DON'T PANIC

One of the most important lessons all my adventures have taught me is the importance of keeping fear and panic firmly locked away in a steel chest where they can't do too much damage. These emotions are worse than just a waste of energy and time. They are debilitating forces that will keep your mind from seeing or thinking clearly, being productive, or actually making headway toward solving whatever emergency, crisis, or tough spot you're in. Panic and fear are the enemy, and you need to treat them as such.

But how do you battle an enemy you can't see? The

first step is to recognize and name it for what it is. Why do we panic or feel fear when we're about to leap off a cliff, or find ourselves in the middle of uncertain and challenging circumstances? *Because we fear something bad might happen.* The challenge might defeat us. We might not be able to pay the bills. We might not survive the loneliness or sorrow. We might not recover from that tragedy. The future might be worse than the past. But when you really look at it, all of these paralyzing fears stems from one big, ugly fear: that we might not be strong enough to handle what awaits us around that blind curve in the road. We might fail. We might break. We might not be *enough*.

So what do you do about that? The first thing is to remember that the fear of something is almost always worse than the thing itself. Humans are remarkably resilient. We cope far better than we think we will with all sorts of challenges, tragedies, and discomfort. Fear only exists in the future. In the present, we cope, heal, learn, and move on. We find a way. So if you start to feel fear creeping up on you, remember to ask yourself: "Am I okay right now?" If the answer's yes, take a deep breath and focus on coming up with either a) a list of factual reasons why that scary future isn't really likely or b) a plan or plans that will keep that imagined scary future from coming to pass.

Beyond that, there are some coping mechanisms that can help. The first involves sheer discipline of the mind. I discovered this the hard way, flying my airplane over the North Carolina mountains one time when the haze was thicker than reported and I lost all outside visual references or hint of a horizon. The problem was, I'm not certified to fly only on instruments, in the clouds. All pilots get emergency training in instrument flying, but that doesn't make you really good at it. And without any visual reference points, vertigo sets in within seconds. You'll think you're flying straight and level, and you're actually in a steep, descending bank—which is probably what killed John F. Kennedy, Jr.

But as I flew along, focusing desperately on my instruments to keep my airplane level until I got out of the mountains, where the visibility was supposed to be better, I discovered that the task of flying the airplane on instruments wasn't my biggest problem. My biggest challenge—the thing that was really going to kill me—was my mind. All I had to do was keep the airplane straight and level until things got better, and I actually knew how to do that. But I also knew I was in a tough spot. And as the minutes dragged on, my fear that I might fail at my life-and-death task mounted. "This is how pilots die," a frightened voice started echoing inside my head. "You're not qualified to do this. How long can you keep this up? What if you can't do it?" And as that voice got louder, my performance started to deteriorate. The wings dipped. My altitude and speed wavered. My hands got shaky, and my breath became ragged.

Fortunately, I recognized the enemy in time. If I wanted to survive, I had to stuff my fear back in the baggage compartment. I could not allow those fearful thoughts anywhere near my conscious mind. So any time I felt myself starting to doubt, I willfully shoved the thought out of my mind. "Giving up is not an option!" I said to myself, over and over. "Fear is not going to win today! I will focus, and I will fly this plane!"

Sounds silly, but it worked.

"Action is the antidote to despair."

— JOAN BAEZ

2

Keep Moving

My experience over the mountains of North Carolina taught me something else, as well. Panic and fear set in faster and stronger if you feel helpless about your situation—or if you're sitting still. Most consequences aren't quite as severe as the ones I was facing that day. But whatever the challenge you're facing … if you start feeling yourself overwhelmed (a mild version of panic that usually comes with a nagging, fearful voice that's very sure you won't manage your challenges successfully, but which can lead to full-blown panic), force yourself to focus on *doing something*. Maybe the big challenge is too much to figure out. But there's generally *something* productive you can do, no matter how small, that will make you feel like you're making some progress forward. You may not know how you're going to find your way home. But you can gather wood for a small fire, so you don't freeze when the sun goes down. Build some shelter. Think about a plan for the morning. Action focuses the mind, and a focused, busy mind is less susceptible to the demons of discouragement, fear, and panic.

Action also has the added benefit of changing your inertia. An object at rest tends to stay at rest. Talk to any mountain climber about how important it is, when the weather gets bad and the going gets rough, to *keep going*. The longer you sit, the harder it is to move at all. But once you're moving, the path of least resistance is to keep moving. And if you keep moving long enough, you'll get somewhere. As a friend of mine says, "let's do *something*, even if it's something wrong. We can always correct course. But we can't even do that if we don't move in *some* direction first." And sometimes, even if your first direction isn't the right one, it may lead you to stumble across an answer, or a contact, or an important tool that helps get you where you eventually want or need to go.

"Nothing is a life and death situation—except life, and death."

—Nancy Boersma

3

KEEP PERSPECTIVE

Another critical tool—not only for keeping panic at bay, but also for enjoying all the gifts and benefits adventures also contain—is to keep things in perspective. One of the best gifts I've gotten from flying is the perspective it gives me—not only on the world itself, but of what really matters, in the scheme of things. When I'm flying, the consequences for a mistake can be fatal. But while that can be stressful when I'm in the middle of an in-flight emergency, it has the advantage of putting all the other life problems I encounter in their proper perspective. Anytime I start feeling scared about how something in my life is going to turn out, I ask myself, "What's the worst thing that happens here? Does anyone die?" If the answer is "no," I ratchet the worry down a few notches. No cause is really lost as long as you live to fight another day.

Spending some time close to the edge also reminds you, in no uncertain terms, of what really matters in life. And flat-screen TVs, big houses, designer pocketbooks—and even many more routine comforts and luxuries in life—aren't on the list. We get attached to things, unless we're at risk of losing people. Then those things become far less important. So, you have to sell the big house. That sounds terrible, unless you consider whose shoes you'd rather be in ... those, or those of a parent whose child has just been diagnosed with a brain tumor. Easy to say, I know. And as a friend of mine succinctly puts it, "just because the guy in the bed next to you has an amputated leg, it doesn't make your broken ankle hurt any less."

But, still. Keeping in mind not only that other people have it worse, but also all that you still *have*—and where those things rate on a scale of merely nice, to important, to *really* important—can do a lot toward maintaining a good, healthy sense of perspective in the middle of uncertainty or a tough, life-changing adventure. And having spent time in both third world countries and on uncomfortable, rustic adventures, I will say that it's surprising what material items you can be happy without.

Keeping perspective can also be a matter of revisiting what you thought was important or took for granted as part of your life. Do you really need that extra car, or the dinners out, if giving them up can allow you to pursue a more fulfilling career? What matters to you more? Uncertain times are useful, because they force you to look harder at those questions than you otherwise might. And the answers you come up with might surprise you. They also might liberate you in ways you never thought possible.

"I seldom end up where I wanted to go, but almost always end up where I need to be."

—Douglas Adams

4

Embrace Your Freedom

Nothing makes an adventure or journey more miserable than spending it wishing you were somewhere else. Most of us have had at least one unfortunate encounter with a poor traveling companion who made us want to pitch them off a convenient bridge or ledge, because they spent the entire trip complaining. From the outside, we can see clearly that our companion is missing the fun of the trip by focusing only on what it doesn't offer, but it's harder to keep that perspective when you're in the middle of an uncertain adventure, yourself.

Yet, as a friend of mine once put it, "If life suddenly

shunts the train you're on from Track A to Track B, you can't force it back onto Track A. You're on a different track—at least for a while. But if you spend the whole trip wishing you were on Track A, you'll miss whatever Track B had to offer. And Track B might have wonderful scenery you would have missed if life had turned out the way you wanted it to."

So to the best of your ability, try to let go of where you're *not*, and focus on what opportunities and advantages might be found where you *are*. You might be surprised at what you discover. Truth to tell, one of the big reasons I've gotten out and explored as much of the world as I have is because my life didn't go the way I expected or wanted it to. I spent a lot of my 30s worrying about finding a guy to settle down with. But as I approached 40, I realized that there were actually some wonderful advantages to being single and unencumbered. I could go spend a month or more in Africa, Europe, Asia or Australia without missing someone at home, and without feeling guilty about leaving kids or family alone. "Embrace your freedom," my mother had said. And so I decided to do just that. I would travel as much as I could—mostly in connection with writing assignments—while I had the freedom to do that. Then if someone came along I wanted to settle down with, or who had children or a life that made it more difficult to travel, I wouldn't feel like I'd missed out on seeing the world. And if they didn't … well, exploring the world sure beat sitting around wishing I had something I didn't.

"*Even Noah got no salary for the first six months. Partly on account of the weather and partly because he was learning navigation.*"

—MARK TWAIN

5

Navigate, Evaluate, Innovate

Navigating an uncharted adventure or hero's journey, with no map and no guide, is a tricky proposition. It's why more people don't do it. And yet, if you learn how to navigate well without those things, you can become as strong as a seasoned sea captain who knows how to read the wind and can steer a true course through any uncertain storm or sea.

How do you get that skill? Mostly through the hard but effective school of experience. One of the greatest challenges of any uncharted journey is the pressure of constantly having to decide where to go next. Ask any adventurer which is harder—the decision to act, or acting on that decision, and they will undoubtedly say that the decision itself is the more difficult task. After that, it's just implementation and tenacity until you have to re-evaluate or come to the next decision point.

But how do you make the right decision? It's part analysis and experimentation, and part intuition. Think about sailors setting off across an uncharted sea. They might have a general destination or direction in mind. But they can't say, at the start, exactly how they're going to get there. Or even if they're going to end up where they initially thought they would. They might start out on a northwesterly course. But they might travel a little distance in that direction and realize they need to tack southwest for a while, first. As they gain experience, they'll probably get better at working with the prevailing winds and judging what different currents and water conditions mean. So they'll probably spend less time on unproductive tacks or course headings.

But as any adventurer, explorer, artist or entrepreneur will tell you—a lot of the time, you have to try an approach or direction for a bit before you can tell if it's the right one. So the key is to proceed with a certain amount of watchful caution. Experimentation is necessary and great, but try to experiment in such a way that mistakes aren't calamitous. Take, for example, my dilemma when I got stranded on the glacier in my tennis shoes and shorts. I didn't know what approach was going to work best, in terms of getting down the slope. So I experimented … but with *little steps*, so if my approach didn't work, I wouldn't instantly lose my balance and fall the rest of the way.

"*I believe that there is a subtle magnetism in Nature, which, if we unconsciously yield to it, will direct us aright.*"

—Henry David Thoreau

6

SWIM DOWNSTREAM

Another key to navigating unknown waters successfully is learning how to read prevailing winds and currents, and then learning to work *with* them, instead of against them. If you feel like you're running into one immovable and frustrating obstacle after another, you may be trying to kayak upstream—which, as any river kayaker can tell you, is the fastest way to end up upside down and sideways, with your head banging against an underwater rock. In river kayaking, the key to success is to find and work with the prevailing currents. And the same is true in life. I've had far more success pursuing those doors that seemed to fly open in front of me, instead of stubbornly banging away at paths that offered frustration at every turn—even if that's turned the course of my adventures and life away from where I planned or wanted to go.

In 2001, I went to Africa to write an article on flying a bush airplane in the game parks of Kenya. Everything that could go wrong *did* go wrong, including the fact that the airplane I was supposed to fly never cleared customs in the port of Mombasa. I kept trying to make that story work, despite the frustrations and ugly turns of events. That was my assignment, after all. But the process was excruciating. I eventually got something of a story done, but it wasn't anything memorable.

In the midst of all that, however, I bumped into a couple of pilots in a café in Nairobi who immediately began trying to convince me to go flying with them. I asked them if they flew in the game parks. No, they said, they were flying relief supplies into Sudan. A story on flying relief supplies into Sudan was the furthest thing from my mind. But after having banged my head against bureaucratic and personal nightmare walls for three weeks, here were two pilots eager to fly with me somewhere. I decided to follow the current ... which is how I ended up flying into a civil war, for one thing. But the time I spent with those pilots was the most educational and worldview-changing of my life. And that story led to another whole trip to Africa, pursuing far more interesting stories than the one I initially went to Africa to write.

"Look at every path closely and deliberately. Then ask yourself, and yourself alone, one question: Does this path have a heart? If it does, the path is good. If it doesn't, it is of no use."

—Carlos Castaneda

7

TRUST THE FORCE

In addition to reading currents and learning from experimentation, there's another element that all good sea captains and adventurers incorporate into their decisions. Call it intuition, call it the unconscious result of our supercomputer brains taking in all available experience and information and integrating it into a visceral answer, or call it The Force—it's an internal compass that's very rarely wrong. And it's something every epic hero learns to use in order to successfully navigate their way through the risks and obstacles of their journey. They consider the known risks and facts about each potential path or choice.

But they also try to sense which path or choice "feels" less resistant and more "right." It's what a surfer does when searching for the "groove" on a wave, what Luke Skywalker did when opening himself to guidance from "The Force," or a Yaqui Warrior does when asking whether a particular path has "heart."

One of the biggest turning points in my career occurred after a tough stretch of about four years where I'd had to sell my first airplane and concentrate completely on making enough money to survive as a writer. I finally saved enough money so I could either buy another airplane and get back into flying, or put a really good down payment on a condo in Los Angeles, where I was living at the time.

Believe it or not, it was a tough choice to make. Predictably, most of my LA friends came down firmly on the side of the condo. They pointed out that real estate was a better investment, and that condos had the advantage of being more comfortable places to sleep. Not to mention having a far lower risk of crashing. I was also approaching my late 30s. Buying an airplane instead of a place to live at that age seemed almost embarrassingly irresponsible.

The only problem was that when I tried to picture owning and living in a condo in Santa Monica, or buying a plane and getting back into flying again, the only image that felt happy was buying the plane. So I bought it. Not without heartburn, or butterflies in my stomach, or night fears that I might be making one of the bigger and more expensive mistakes of my life. But it *felt* right. So I bought the plane and told myself I'd just see what happened.

What *happened* was that two weeks later, I got a call from the editor-in-chief of *Flying* magazine—the top magazine in the industry; the magazine every aviation writer dreamed of working for. He wanted to talk about having me write for the magazine, but he had one question first: Did I own an airplane? Because, he said, he didn't want anyone writing for the magazine who didn't own their own airplane.

The world works in mysterious ways. And while charting your own course opens up an infinitely larger field of possibilities, navigating through unmarked territory can sometimes feel like trying to figure out what you want to order from a 500-page menu. It also carries the extra pressure of knowing that the decisions you make will materially affect your life, with the added frustration of never getting to know how the path you *didn't* choose might have turned out.

But the good news is, there is rarely a single "right" path or course in life. Even epic heroes often end up someplace other than where they expected to be. Which is why the Yaqui warrior saying is so powerful. Where we end up is far less important than whether the path we're on is fulfilling. If it is, we'll be happy. Even if the scenery looks a little different than we thought it would.

"One cannot discover new lands without consenting to lose sight of the shore for a very long time."

—ANDRE GIDE

8

REMEMBER THE NIGHT IS DARKEST
RIGHT BEFORE THE DAWN

Hero journeys are adventures through the forest of the unknown. There will be obstacles, choices, and risks. There will be times when you reach a ridgeline and see the distant horizon you hope to reach, awash in sun and glory. And there will be times, deep in the shadows of the valleys, when you'll be hard-pressed to see two feet through the trees and fog surrounding you. After several years of self-employment, I finally decided that faith wasn't going forward onto an unknown path. It was going forward when you couldn't see a path at all. Faith was trusting that ground would appear underneath your feet if you had the courage to step forward into the mist.

But how do you get through the dark nights of doubt when that faith gets shaky? For one thing is certain: if you're really on a hero's journey, there *will* be those times. Especially when a direction you've tried turns out to be a dead end, or the pressures of finances or competing needs pile up and threaten to topple over on your head.

First … remember it's a hero's journey. The dark nights of the soul, where you find yourself questioning everything, can lead you to explore, establish or reaffirm the things that matter most to you, and who you are at the core. No hero becomes truly strong without going through that process. After all, being strong isn't a matter of never falling down. Every epic hero, and every human being, falls down. It's how you learn to get back up that matters. And the more honest and open you are with yourself, the more strength you'll have to do that.

But the dark moments are also where doing the work of finding and following a "path with heart" can really pay off. Someone asked me once, at a speech I gave, whether it was true that if you did what you loved, the money would follow. I thought about that for a moment and answered, "Well, yes, but not the way you're thinking." Because if you find something you love to do, then in those dark moments of doubt, when you question whether you're crazy, or whether you're going to end up living on a Lexington Avenue subway grate ... if your bottom-line answer to the question, "Does this path have heart?" is, "Yes. I am doing what I most want to do; something that feeds my heart and soul and *matters* in the world" ... then you become motivated to move Heaven and Earth in order to keep from giving that path up. You *find* a way to keep going; to keep enough money coming in to keep the boat afloat.

"One of my associates, after we had conducted the crowning experiment and it had proved a failure, expressed discouragement and disgust over our having failed to find out anything. I cheerily assured him that we had learned something. For we had learned for a certainty that the thing couldn't be done that way, and that we would have to try some other way."

—THOMAS EDISON

9

Learn from your Mistakes

One of the biggest demon fears any of us have when starting out on an adventure or journey is the fear of failure. I struggle with it daily. But here's the thing. Failure is an integral part of experimentation and exploration. And it can be incredibly educational, as long as you analyze it for what it can tell you, instead of just shying away from it in embarrassment.

In the world of Silicon Valley, venture capitalists say that they don't view entrepreneurs who've had a previous business fail as tainted. They look instead at what those people have learned from the experience, because they know that sometimes, failure is the best way to figure out what *not* to do in the future.

I know all too well what they mean. The examples of my failures are almost as numerous and varied as any successes I've ever had. Once, I spent the better part of 18 months trying to write and sell a screenplay. I wrote 11 drafts of a screenplay that didn't sell. And as it turns out, I don't think I'm particularly gifted as a screenwriter. So was the time wasted? No. I learned some useful things about storytelling, for starters. But more importantly, I now know that I don't want to do that kind of writing, so I don't feel tempted to pursue that gold ring anymore. Which is actually quite liberating, and a big help in focusing my talents elsewhere.

It would be nice, of course, to be able to look ahead and figure out the best course or choice before trying it out for a while—the best job to take, the outfit that will really prove worth the money you spent on it, or the couch that will look best in your living room. But if we were all so talented at figuring things out ahead of time, there wouldn't be such a thing as "return" departments … or divorce, or consignment stores, or clauses that let us drop university classes partway through a semester. Sometimes, even when we're not in the middle of an adventure, we try things that don't work, and we don't figure that out until a few miles down the road.

But blazing your own trail through an uncertain forest, where there's less guidance to tell you what the consequences of a particular choice will be, means some wrong turns are almost inevitable. After all, a hero's journey is all about learning along the way. But what's important to remember is: what differentiates epic heroes from more tragic characters is that they *learn* from their mistakes. That learning, and that willingness to adjust their view of themselves and the course they take through the world, is what allows the hero to emerge on the far side of the dark nights and difficult battles triumphant, with the strength of tempered steel.

"No man is an Island, entire of itself; every man is a piece of the Continent, a part of the main."

—John Donne

10

SEEK AND NURTURE FRIENDS AND KINDRED SPIRITS

One of the most important elements in any epic hero journey tale is the role played by the friends and unexpected guides who appear along the way. Where would Frodo Baggins have been without his good friend Sam? Or Gandalf? Or the enchanted trees, for that matter? Many epic heroes begin by thinking they can conquer the world on their own. None succeed without letting go of that notion, even if they recognize that there are battles—particularly internal battles—we all have to work through on our own.

That rule also holds true for more than just epic hero

tales. We may nurture a cultural myth of pioneering self-reliance here in America, but the truth is … few of those pioneers could have survived without the help of others to raise their barns, defend against attackers, or form a fire brigade. And that's not even getting into emotional support friends and community offer when times are dark or sad.

The most valuable friends and guides, however, are those who are kindred spirits; who understand what it is we're trying to accomplish and back us all the way. Not blindly, but with the loyalty of Sam, and the supportive encouragement of Amy Madigan's character in *Field of Dreams*, who tells her husband that if he really feels he should plow under a field of corn to build a baseball diamond, then he should do it, even if it's a crazy idea. For there will be plenty of others who tell us we're being irresponsible or nuts.

Part of the challenge of a hero's journey, in fact, is to hold true to course in the face of little support from the outside world. Because if you're really on an uncharted hero's journey, you probably won't get a ton of understanding or support from people who are firmly attached to their well-known village lives or following only clearly defined roads. As a greeting card I once found said, "Those who hear not the music think the dancers mad."

A hero's journey can be lonely, because it involves walking away from the comfort others are still clinging to, even if you didn't choose the events that forced you out of that comfort. There will be times when you have to accept that others just don't understand. So be careful whom you ask for support. Many will be unable to provide it. But the flip side of that is … in the dark woods and night of a hero's journey tale, after the hero has walked away from the villagers who can't follow, or don't understand, there are always fellow travelers; kindred spirits who appear to keep the hero company and help protect and guide them. That's not just a fairy tale idea. It's how the world works.

Every major break I've had in my career has had the assisting fingerprints of some friend, mentor, or magically appearing guide on it somewhere. Sometimes, the link has been obvious. The editor of *Flying* magazine didn't just call me out of the blue. He called because a mutual friend, who knew my work and knew I'd just bought an airplane, put the two of us together. At other times, the assistance has appeared as unexpectedly as a lady rising from a lake with a silver sword in her hand.

Several years after I got the column at *Flying*, after trying without success to expand my writing and contacts into the more mainstream publishing world, I got an email from a reader who said he was a huge fan of my "literary writing in *Flying*" and wanted to talk to me about expanding my writing from there. I scrolled down to the signature line. The email was from the publisher of *Forbes* magazine. Who, it turned out, just happened to be a pilot. And who has since become a good friend.

I don't know why or how that kind of thing happens. But I've come to accept the fact that it does. If you stay true to the hero's course, and keep working hard to make forward progress, then no matter how dark the night gets at times ... the dawn comes; the guides appear. The epic hero journey tales may be apocryphal, but the elements endure because they've proven themselves over centuries of human effort. Keep the faith, be a good friend, learn to ask for help when you need it, and build a network of kindred spirits ... and somehow, you'll make it through.

"The aim of life is to live, and to live means to be aware, joyously, drunkenly, serenely, divinely aware."

—HENRY MILLER

11

ENJOY THE VIEW

Believe it or not, there will come a time when life is settled again and the wildest part of the adventure or journey is behind you (unless you make seeking adventure a life path in and of itself). And when you're safely employed again, or hugely successful in your business, or back home from the Alps, with its breathtaking expanses of snow and glacial ice out of reach once more ... it'd be a shame if you'd been so focused on just trudging across the snowfields that you didn't stop to take any pictures, or look around and recognize just how exciting and beautiful it all was at the time.

For, despite all the discomfort and uncertainty it entails, an adventure or hero's journey will also take places—within yourself and in your life—that you may not visit again. So take the time to look for, and appreciate, the gifts and moments that liven up the journey along the way. When I was getting ready to leave on one of my long, solo cross-country airplane trips, a friend of mine said to me, "Just remember ... sometimes you have to stop and remind yourself you're having fun. Otherwise you can get so wrapped up in the work and stress of flying that you miss it."

Sounds ridiculous, but it's true. No matter where you are, take time to be alive in that moment, for it will not come again. Breathe. Look around. Be aware. Be appreciative. And laugh, as often as you can.

VIII

THE RETURN

Regardless of whether the journey was a temporary adventure or a more prolonged hero's journey ... it isn't complete unless you return back home again. But what does that mean? In some cases—a search for a new job, or a physical adventure of climbing a mountain—there's a clear end-point. Eventually, you find a job or get back home. But often, the "Return" of a hero's journey isn't so clear-cut, because the Return is that moment when you learn the lessons the journey had to offer, and you both *recognize* whatever strength, skills, and understanding your trials and experiences have conferred upon you and start *applying* them to your life going forward. It's the moment of transformation of perspective; when change and uncertainty cease to be frightening, and you realize you've become somehow stronger.

No one can predict exactly when that moment will occur, and a certain amount of patience, perseverance, and determined effort is involved. But there are some things you can do to aid in the dawning of that enlightenment and enhance its impact. Here are just a few:

"What have you learned, Dorothy?"

—HICKORY/THE TIN MAN
THE WIZARD OF OZ

1

TAKE NOTES AND REFLECT

It's a fairly well-documented fact that human beings do not remember pain very clearly—at least, in the sense of being able to call up the actual sensation of pain after the fact. This lapse may account for why women are willing to undergo subsequent pregnancies even after enduring the wrenching pain of childbirth. But the truth is, sensations are fleeting things. We might remember that we felt a certain way, but we don't, or can't, hold onto the vivid experience of that feeling after the fact. Even when we try.

I recently had the opportunity to fly in an Air Force

U-2 spy plane more than 70,000 feet above the planet. It was a once-in-a-lifetime opportunity, requiring a space suit, a week of training, and two and a half years of effort to win approval for the flight to even take place. From the lofty heights of that fragile altitude, most of the atmosphere is beneath you, and you can actually see the curvature of the Earth. The sky fades from midnight blue to black above you, and the planet beneath you appears to be at once a massive rock and a breathtakingly fragile ecosystem, protected by an impossibly thin cushion of survivable atmospheric "air."

You would *think* that being immersed in a world so dramatic—and so dramatically different from anything I'd seen or experienced before—would etch the details and sensations of that flight into my memory with unforgettable clarity. But, no. There are *moments* I still recall clearly—mostly because, in between all the tasks I had to manage, I made a conscious effort to quiet my mind, sit back, and take in my surreal surroundings. "Remember this!" I repeated fiercely to myself as I tried to mentally catalogue the sensations and sights of the moment.

But the reason I could write the vivid description at

the beginning of this anecdote about the world as I saw it there is because I've learned, over the years, that just making mental notes isn't enough. The sensations fade and our brains move on, overwriting the sharp emotions and thoughts of the moment with new events and thoughts—and an inescapable shift in perspective.

So before I got in the plane, I told the pilot that I'd need a way to take written notes up there. This would be no mean feat at minus 60 degrees centigrade, where pen ink tends to congeal, and encased in a Michelin-man pressure suit and gloves. But the Air Force technicians provided me with two easily-accessible, sharpened pencils and a legal-sized wooden board, on which they'd taped two light green pieces of paper. As amazing as the experience was, it was by re-reading my clumsily and almost illegibly-scribbled random thoughts and feelings, recorded real-time, that I was able to pull back the details of the experience and mine them for additional insights and perspective.

Granted, a U-2 flight is a bit extreme, both in terms of experience and difficulty in note-taking. But the point is equally true regardless of what kind of adventure I'm experiencing. No matter how sharp the pain, joy or crisis of the moment, it blurs unless I write down my thoughts, feelings, arguments, questions, and potential answers real-time—or at least, as close to real-time as I can get.

Why does that matter? Obviously, we all like to remember the great moments and scenic landscapes of our lives. It's why we take vacation and wedding photos. But why on earth would anyone want to make an effort to remember painful feelings of being afraid or discouraged, or exhausting struggles to find a path in the fog?

Two reasons. First, there are valuable lessons of growth, self-knowledge, insight and truth to be gleaned from those moments of challenge and adventure. And second, those lessons often can only be mined successfully with the perspective of hindsight. I firmly believe there are lessons to be gained from almost all of life's experiences. But often, it takes me a little bit of time—and sometimes a *lot* of time—to be able to see them clearly. And in order to go back and evaluate my emotions, thoughts, and experiences after the fact, I have to have some way of reaching them again. Hence the importance of taking notes.

Of course, to take any worthwhile notes, we first have to be aware. And self-aware. Which means acting as an observer as well as a participant in the adventure. Explorers used to bring along scribes to document their journeys. In our own life adventures, we typically don't have that luxury. We have to act as our own thoughtful correspondents to the ages, recording our physical, emotional, and mental journeys for future study.

Yet equally important as the actual recording of events is questioning what all that data and recorded material *tells* us. The Tin Man's famous last line in *The Wizard of Oz*—"What have you learned, Dorothy?"—is probably the clunkiest, two-by-four-between-the-eyes tactic ever used by a filmmaker to make sure his audience got the lesson and point of his movie. But the question itself is an important one.

To reap the wisdom of our experiences, we sometimes have to actively seek the kernels of truth they contain. "What did that tell me?" "What do I now know about myself—or people, or life, or adventure, or anything—that I didn't before?" "What have I learned?" are all important questions to ask. And often, we have to ask them over and over again, across time. Because unlike the Hollywood neatness of Dorothy's answer to the Tin Man, we rarely have our final answer—if, in fact, we ever get a "final" answer—right away. Our thoughts and insights often evolve over time. And sometimes they don't even come into focus until we've traveled a lot farther down the road.

"We shall not cease from exploration

And the end of all our exploring

Will be to arrive where we started

And know the place for the first time"

—T.S. ELIOT

2

REMEMBER GROWTH HAPPENS SLOWLY

I've often said to friends that patience is a virtue ... that I do not naturally possess. Every ounce of it I can now draw on was hard-won through discipline and effort. Anytime I've found myself miserable where I was, I've tended to throw myself into a high-energy, forced march through the forest in order to change my circumstances, no matter how difficult or uncertain the way. Not because I'm exceptionally industrious, but because I want the sunlight of clarity and change *now*. Or if I can't have it now, then as soon as humanly possible.

Unfortunately, change and growth do not happen

instantly, or even quickly. When exactly, for example, does winter turn to spring, or does a baby acquire the skills necessary to walk? Not in any particular moment you can point to, although there may be a moment when we become *aware* that a shift has occurred.

The same is true for learning. Someone told me once that there are four stages of learning. In the first stage, you don't know what you don't know (otherwise known as the bliss of ignorance). In the second stage, you know what you don't know (usually after stumbling and realizing something is harder than you thought). In the third stage, you don't know what you know. You've learned enough to acquire a fair amount of skill in a particular area, but you don't have confidence in the full strength of that skill yet. In the last stage, you know what you know. This is mastery, and the awareness of it usually dawns gradually over time and experience, or in a flash of insight when your skills get severely tested and you realize you actually met the challenge surprisingly well.

Think of Luke Skywalker. He'd been acquiring skills and knowledge throughout his journey in the first *Star Wars* movie. But it was the final assault on the Death

Star, where his ability to marshal the power of The Force was severely tested, that he gained the confidence in his ability to wield the power of a Jedi Knight. And in that moment—the moment of The Return—the lens through which he saw himself and the world shifted. In a hero's Return, home itself doesn't change. It's the hero's view and understanding of it that does. But that moment of shifting focus—of knowing what we know, and the change in perspective and confidence that accompanies that knowledge—can be weeks, months, or even years in the making.

This point is relevant, because in the midst of an adventure or hero's journey, you may not realize how much you're learning or what new skills you're acquiring—either because you're still learning, or because you simply haven't gotten to the point yet where you know what you know. But have faith. If you're really navigating uncertain, uncharted waters, you *are* learning. You're gaining skills, knowledge, and understanding that will serve you well down the road. Even if it's only to tell you that you don't want to try certain roads or activities again.

But if you keep going, you *will* move along that

progression of knowledge and learning. And one day, you will be tested and proven, or you'll simply wake up and notice that the season has changed. You'll realize that somewhere along the way, you've become a master navigator, a stronger warrior, and a successful captain of your own ship and destiny.

Does that mean you will then win every battle and overcome every obstacle from that day forward? No. But your world, and your view of both the world and yourself, will never be quite the same again.

"The final thing is knowing, loving, and serving life in a way in which you are eternally at rest."

—JOSEPH CAMPBELL

3

APPLY WHAT YOU'VE LEARNED

So you finish the adventure, get the new job, reach the mountaintop, defeat the Death Star, and gain new levels of understanding about your strengths and the world. The journey is over, right?

No. *One* journey or chapter may be over. But life is a never-ending series of chapters. Any student of Hollywood sequels understands this basic truth. *The Empire Strikes Back*, and all that. As the Greek philosopher Heraclitus wrote, "everything flows, nothing stands still … and nothing endures but change."

Uncertainty will always be a part of life. New

challenges, adventures, and journeys will present themselves for as long as we live. So the hero's real challenge is to bring the holy grail *back*; to bring the knowledge, strength, and wisdom acquired in the initiation journey back and integrate it into a life lived more fully and wisely from that day forward. If that doesn't happen, the journey isn't complete, and the hero is not a true hero.

The trick to the Return is to figure out how to *apply* all of what you've learned—both to enhance your life and allow you to keep a more serene center in the face of future adventures, journeys, or storms. As French author René Daumal wrote in the unfinished novel *Mount Analogue*, "There is an art to finding your way in the lower regions by the memory of what you have seen when you were higher up. When you can no longer see, you can at least still know."

The true hero's journey, in other words ... is the ongoing one.

CONCLUSION

One of the worst feelings in the world is helplessness. In a series of classic experiments conducted in the 1950s, dogs in two rooms were subjected to electric shocks. In one room, the shock was preceded by a tone, and the dog could stop the shock by hitting a button or lever. In the other room, the shock came unannounced, and the dog had no way of stopping it. After a time, the two dogs were put into another room, where there was a low barrier. Again, a tone sounded, and a shock was given. But the dog who'd had the lever in the previous experiment soon learned that it could stop these new shocks by jumping over the barrier. In short order, the dog would jump over the barrier as soon as the tone sounded, bypassing the shock altogether. But the other dog—the one who'd learned that it couldn't affect what was happening to it—never even attempted to jump the barrier in the second experiment. It just lay down and whimpered when the tone sounded and the shock began.

One of the reasons that uncertain times are so scary is that we—like that second dog—fear that it means bad things will happen to us, and there will be nothing we can do to prevent or stop them. We feel helpless in the face of the economic or global forces creating all that uncertainty. And helplessness is depressing.

But the truth is, we have far more power to control our lives than we sometimes think. And that, more than anything else, is the lesson and message of the hero's journey. One of my favorite T-shirt designs (created by the talented folks at a company called WomenFly) shows a pair of ruby red slippers reflected in a pair of barnstormer goggles. Next to the image, it says, "Dorothy had the shoes, but she didn't have the vision. Take the controls. *Women Fly*."

When routine collapses—either because we've willingly stepped into an adventure or hero's journey, or because life has thrown us there without asking our opinion or permission—we have more than just an opportunity to change direction. We have the opportunity to seize the controls and prove we can find our own way home, wizard or no wizard. We have the opportunity to grab hold of life with two hands and learn just how strong we really are. We have the opportunity to become not just who we settled for, but all we're capable of being.

That doesn't mean the process is easy. It's not. Adventure, after all, is rarely comfortable, and nothing worthwhile ever came without some kind of effort, heartache or risk. But the reason hero journey tales endure over the centuries is that their message is so powerful. Yes, they say, life is uncertain. And yes, the process of learning how to survive and thrive in the midst of all that uncertainty and challenge is difficult. But they also argue that none of us are helpless, no matter what the world throws at us, unless we choose to act that way; that we all have the potential power and strength of a hero inside of us—if only we find the courage to seize the controls of our lives and step out bravely into the world.

A woman named Robyn Davidson set out, at the age of 27, to travel solo across the desert wilderness of the Australian Outback by camel. One doesn't have to have much of an imagination to guess that the trip was a far cry from comfortable. But Davidson said the experience taught her, "You are as strong and powerful as you allow yourself to be."

Navigating uncertain or unknown circumstances is never entirely comfortable. But if you look at it as an opportunity and adventure, it can be creative, energizing, and even liberating. It can wake up your senses and remind you how it feels to be alive again. It can force you to do some important prioritizing and housecleaning—in both your mind and your life. It can open up new horizons and allow you to find a more fulfilling path. It might even give you back a little of the energy and passion you had when you were young and believed in limitless possibilities.

But most importantly, it can give you an opportunity to learn that you can find your way home, even without a map or guide. The reward of the journey is The

Return—that moment when the heroes realize that home and security are not tied to a place or set of circumstances, but that home is a state of being, and their security lies within themselves. Why? Because they've learned they have the strength to endure, persevere, and prevail, no matter what the circumstances.

It's heady stuff. But it also has the advantage, as they say, of being true. By embracing uncertainty, and diving into the adventure it holds, you will gain many gifts. But perhaps the most powerful is simply this: once you climb a mountain, no hill will ever seem so tall again. That inner freedom—from fear, from a feeling of helplessness, from imaginary limits that bind our hearts or lives—is the hero's true reward. And it's waiting out there for all of us to find.

ABOUT THE AUTHOR

Lane Wallace is a correspondent for *TheAtlantic.com* and an internationally-known aviation columnist. Her work has also appeared in *The New York Times*, *ForbesLife*, *The Dallas Morning News*, and *Elite Traveler*, in addition to numerous other publications. Her blog, *No Map. No Guide. No Limits.* (www.nomapnoguidenolimits.com), focuses on taking a more adventurous, entrepreneurial, and passion-inspired approach to life.

If Wallace knows a thing or two about adventure, it's because she left a successful corporate career 20 years ago to become an adventure writer and pilot. Since then, she's climbed mountains in Nepal and Europe, kayaked the Na Pali Coast of Hawaii, gone wreck diving in French Polynesia, and explored glaciers in Alaska. Her adventures have also included flying relief supplies in both the Amazon jungle and conflict zones in Africa, as well as donning a space suit to fly an Air Force U-2 above 70,000 feet.

Lane has been interviewed on NPR, BBC, CBC and other radio and television outlets and has spoken about adventure, passion, innovation and surviving uncertainty to a wide variety of audiences, from executive retreats and business conventions to the 92nd Street Y, Stanford University and the Society of Experimental Test Pilots.

In addition to her magazine, newspaper and online writing, Wallace has written six books for NASA on flight and space exploration and worked as a writer and producer on a number of television and video projects. This is her second book about adventure. Her first, *Unforgettable*, is available through Sportys.com.

To learn more, visit www.LaneWallace.com.

29818918R00100

Made in the USA
Lexington, KY
09 February 2014